'UP IS WHERE WE GO FROM HERE'

ROBERT STELL

The essential survival guide for
the small and growing business

bradburystell.co.uk

Matador
9 Priory Business Park
Kibworth Beauchamp
Leicestershire LE8 0RX, UK
Tel: (+44) 116 279 2299
Fax: (+44) 116 279 2277
Email: books@troubador.co.uk
Web: www.troubador.co.uk/matador

ISBN 978 1780881 867

British Library Cataloguing in Publication Data.
A catalogue record for this book is available from the British Library.

Printed in Great Britain by the MPG Books Group, Bodmin and King's Lynn

Matador is an imprint of Troubador Publishing Ltd

CONTENTS

ACKNOWLEDGEMENTS

Without the assistance of Sally Simmons and Judy Watts this book would never have seen the light of day. Their energy, enthusiasm and insight have proved to be nothing short of invaluable.

FOREWORD

Every now and then I find myself going into London to see a client. On one occasion recently I happened to be on a train with all the other morning commuters. I boarded the train at Richmond station as the dawn was beginning to break. No seats were to be found on the train as many of the passengers had already been on it for over an hour from deepest, darkest, Surrey. As I stood there grasping one of the rails I had a chance to look at my fellow commuters. What a sorry sight they looked, some sleeping, some reading, some listening to their i-pods. All grey, listless with the life seemingly sucked out of them, even before they had reached their place of work.

The wage slaves...

Maybe they are actually happy in what they are doing, who knows. One thing I was sure of, I thanked God I wasn't one of them. So you, dear reader, are either someone who is thinking of starting a business or someone who has just started one. My advice to those who are thinking of starting a business is, do it soon, you will never regret it. Your life will be richer and not just in financial terms, and you will be set free. Your journey will not be an easy one and you will know greater highs and greater lows than you've ever known before, but as it is often said, life is not a rehearsal, so do it now. This book is not a get rich quick manual, as I don't think you should ever be reading those kind of books. This is a book to guide you along the lonely road, to give you encouragement and to help you solve some of the problems which you will undoubtedly encounter.

If you have just set up your business, congratulations, you have already joined the elite. The road ahead of you is no doubt going to be a hard one, but it is the road less travelled and the journey will be distinctly more rewarding than the one spent on that commuter train to Waterloo.

This book is set out in an A to Z format, with each letter representing a number of different topics. Throughout the book I will be illustrating and elaborating on these topics with reference to four individuals who have just set up in business (and one very grumpy customer!).

These five characters are:

Heather the Hairdresser

Heather has done a long apprenticeship at a local hairdressers and has now set herself up in her own business, 'Heather's Clip and Snip' on the local high street.

Gary the Gas Engineer

Gary is a Gas Safe registered gas engineer who, having worked for a local firm of (cowboy) engineers, has decided to set up his own boiler and heating engineering firm with an emphasis on quality and integrity.

The Seventy Year Old Mrs Jones

Mrs Jones is one of Gary's customers and is Gary's nemesis. Gary's cocky and chirpy take on life is going to meet its match when he comes face to face with Mrs J... as we shall see.

Simon the Software Engineer

Simon has worked in a City firm developing algorithmic software programmes, specialising in optimisation. Simon is also an extremely keen golfer and has spent many years privately developing a software programme that optimises utilisation of golf courses in association with social media. He has just left his job and is now marketing the software programme full time.

Chris the Consultant

Chris is an IT consultant having worked in a large maintenance company as a hardware engineer. He is very familiar with small business IT networks, the PCs attached to them and the problems that can arise from them. He has set up in business hoping to sell his services by the hour to small and medium size businesses who cannot afford their own in-house IT department.

A... is for Accountants

Of course, I would have to start with this category because that is what I am! And of course, I am doing this at the risk of the reader being turned off immediately. The reality is that you will need an accountant. A good accountant will definitely be your friend and will be worth every penny that you pay him (or her). Do not think for a second that it's all just a load of mumbo jumbo and with on-line filing you can just take care of all of it yourself. You wouldn't consider taking care of your own dental work, and so it is with accountancy. It is a profession and the professionals within it have given up blood, sweat and tears to become qualified and obtain a practising certificate and their advice is worth listening to.

So what should you be looking for when you are choosing your accountant? First of all, you should make sure that he or she is a properly qualified accountant. There are three main branches of the accountancy profession, but a simple question put into Google 'What is a properly qualified accountant?' will reveal to you the letter denominations that you should be looking for. They should not only be fully qualified but they should also have a practising certificate. Do not feel embarrassed about asking for these, and do not assume that because they say they are an accountant they are actually fully qualified. Accountancy, unlike dentistry, medicine, architecture and other professions is not a protected word. Gary, the Gas Engineer could, if he so wished, give up engineering tomorrow and call himself an accountant the day after. In the same way that you wouldn't appoint your mate Jim to be your architect just because he's watched a couple of episodes of Grand Designs, you shouldn't be appointing someone to look after your finances who is not properly qualified to do so.

It would be best to also choose an accountant who has at least some experience of your type of business. Just ask him or her how many other clients he has in that sector. Every business has its own quirks and specifics that the accountant has to be aware of and prior experience is important.

You need to know how much the accountant is going to charge for his services and how often he is going to bill you. In the old days accountants used to only charge by the hour and the answer to the question 'how much are you going to charge?' was... 'it depends'. These days, you should be able to pin down the accountant to a more specific figure. Clearly, the amount of work the accountant does is not absolutely known at the outset, but they should be able to give you an annual cost estimate and that estimate should not differ from the eventual bill by more than £200-£300.

Great Moments in Accountancy

A... is for Advantages

If you want to be a success in business – Be Tall. If you can't be tall Be Funny.

I have read business gurus dolling out advice couched in similar terms i.e. advice that is pointless and unachievable. The point I'm making here is that you need to use your God given advantages.

There is absolutely no doubt that being tall can definitely be used to gain an advantage in business. Chris is 6ft 3in and although sartorially challenged he can still make an impression when walking in a room. That impression would be immeasurably magnified if he were to smarten himself up a bit. A tall, well-dressed man makes a big impact.

Humour is, contrary to what many people may think, extremely useful in business. People who are not in business may think that the making of money is so serious that there is no possible room for humour. Nothing could be further from the truth. If you are funny, use it.

You may have other natural advantages, you may be able to survive on 5 or 6 hours sleep a night, or you may have the ability to work well into the night. Whatever it is be sure to make full use of these advantages.

B

B... is for Banks (and Loans)

Banks are incompetent at everything except theft.

A comment that could get me into serious hot water with the British Bankers Association... except for the fact that the events of 2007/08 have revealed to us (as if we didn't already know) that banks are incompetent on a grand scale.

Sadly, we have no alternative but to use them, as keeping it all under the bed is no longer a viable option. What then can I safely advise you about banks? One thing is that you should try and ensure you are lending them the money and not the other way around. There are of course, fears that banks will go bust again and lose everything but I think those fears are largely unfounded, or at least the risk is extremely small.

Borrowing from banks is an incredibly expensive thing to do and must be done with all due caution. It's not just the interest rate that they will charge (which will be several percent above the base rate) but there will also be an arrangement fee, there will be some charges on the arrangement fee, on the interest on the charges on the fees etc, etc, etc.

Of course, sometimes you will have no alternative and you will have to borrow from a bank. A loan is almost certainly going to be cheaper than an overdraft and an overdraft will be cheaper than borrowing from a credit card. Despite what you may have heard, banks are reluctant to lend to small businesses unless they are themselves protected. In my view this is nothing that you should particularly fear, but a bank will normally ask for the loan to be guaranteed by you personally.

This means that should the loan go bad the bank have the right to take over your personal assets to recover the money. The other way of obtaining a loan is to get it secured against any property that you may have. This could be in the form of a secondary mortgage or a mortgage extension and are known as asset back loans. The shorter the term of these loans clearly the cheaper they are going to be.

Whether you set your business up as a sole trader or a limited company, you will need a separate bank account for your business i.e. separate from your personal bank account. A very simple way to manage your finances on a month to month basis is to set up a monthly transfer from the business account to your personal account, and also a monthly transfer from your business account to a savings account. The latter should be for your tax bill (and clearly therefore must not be touched!), and in very simple terms if you put aside 20% of all the money that you have billed, you will almost certainly have more than enough in that savings account when your accountant writes to you and tells you what your tax bill is going to be. If you have in the end over provided for your tax you can transfer that amount straight back in to the business account. Setting up a bank account is relatively straightforward but will certainly involve an interview with your bank manager. At the time of writing, there is not one single bank that I could recommend over any others, so it is probably best to use your personal bank, as at least they know you.

B... is for Business Plan

The only time you are going to be asked for a business plan is from someone who is going to lend you money or invest directly into your business. What they mean by 'Can I see your business plan' is "When am I going to get my money back?".

The business plan will forecast sales over the coming three to five years depending on the length of the loan you are looking for. You will have to come up with some estimate of costs and of course these must be all well thought out, justified and broken down in very fine detail. Once you have taken the costs away from your sales you will be left with a notional profit, and out of this you will need to repay the loan.

If someone wishes to invest in your business, this means that they are going to get a slice of your equity in exchange for that money. The common mistake people make is to invest in a business and think they are going to get it back in the form of repayments. If you are going to get the money back in the form of repayments this is what is commonly known as a 'loan'. If you are going to invest in someone's business you may get it back and you may not get it back. That is the risk you are taking. What an investor is normally looking for is an exit point sometime in the future. The exit point is when the business is either sold or floated on the stock market. At either of these points the investor will hopefully not only get their money back but also make a profit.

Examples of business plans and how to lay them out may be obtained from The Federation of Small Businesses website: **www.FSB.org.uk.**

B... is for Belief

Belief, resilience and determination are a kind of Holy Trinity of personal characteristics, that if held by one individual will almost certainly propel them to great things. Not all of us are lucky enough to have all three, but to a certain extent all three can be developed. It goes without saying that you have to believe that this business project is going to work, and you have to believe that because this is not going to be easy. You have to shine and polish that belief every single day. I would go as far as saying that it is worth writing down in two or three sentences what these beliefs are. Why you believe that your business has any validity and why do you think that you are going to succeed in this business.

In Heather's case it could be very simple. Heather is quite rightly proud of her skills and she feels the time is right to bring those skills to the market under her own branding. Heather believes she is good at this and she has to keep on believing that.

Events will shake your beliefs and will make you question those beliefs. People can also affect your beliefs. Events are something that you are not going to be able to do anything about but the people that surround you must be primed to know that you need their encouragement.

Simon, despite his confident exterior, is someone whose beliefs and self-esteem can be knocked off course quite quickly. Simon is very fortunate in that his girlfriend tells him every day that his idea is wonderful and he is going to succeed. If Simon didn't have his girlfriend saying that every day there is a good chance that he would pack it all in, as Simon's mother thinks that he is wasting his time and should get down to doing a proper job. Simon should tell his mother to shut up... in the nicest possible way, obviously, but he needs his mother's support and if she is not prepared to give it then the key thing is that she doesn't give Simon any negative thoughts either.

C... is for Contract of Employment

Your business has expanded and you find that you can no longer cope all on your own. The time has come to take on an employee. This is all a little bit scary, because although you may have had experience of hiring people before, when you yourself had a job, hiring someone that you are going to pay out of your own money is an entirely different proposition (See interviewing new staff).

One of the nuts and bolts that you need to be wary of when taking someone on is that they need, by law, to have a contract of employment (this is usually no more than a written statement of main terms of service). They don't need to have this from the very beginning but at least within two months.

If you type in "contracts of employment" into Google you will find many companies who offer standard templates and these can be downloaded for very little money. Once you have downloaded the template you can merely change the details of pay and hours, etc. It may seem like a boring, laborious, bureaucratic task, but will protect both you and the employee and will save a lot of bother in the long run.

C... is for Comfort Zone

The comfort zone is the space where we would all like to be all of the time. As human beings we will always be drawn to the comfort zone. It is our natural inclination. The comfort zone may be the sofa with a cup of tea watching a little bit of breakfast TV before the day begins. It may be a little peek at social networking sites just to get yourself in the mood for work. The reality is that every second you spend in the comfort zone is a second wasted. Further, the longer you procrastinate the harder it is to actually get down to work. Comfort zones are also areas where there is no risk to us, we know that we can stay in that zone and nothing bad is going to happen to us, but in business I'm afraid you have to take yourself out of that comfort zone if you are ever going to succeed.

This could mean standing in front of a new prospect and explaining your new software, going to a networking meeting with a room full of strangers, standing up in public and speaking about your products and services, etc, etc, etc.

There is a phrase 'fortune favours the brave', which I think is largely true. As far as I am aware, there is no phrase 'fortune favours those who sit on the sofa all day'.

C... is for Customer Service

A couple of stories to illustrate just how complicated customer service need not be.

A client of mine who has just had a large extension to his house was recently enthusing to me about his builders. He said they turned up on time on all the days that they said they were going to turn up, they completed the job on time, they didn't swear, they didn't play their radios at full volume and discuss their private lives at equally high volumes and they cleared up after themselves. My client told me that he would recommend them to anybody and urged me to spread the word.

What was interesting about his story was that at no point did he mention the quality of the work, he was purely recommending these builders on the absence of negatives!

I recently received a letter from my electricity supplier and in the middle of the letter was this paragraph:

"Making Electricity Easy

You are currently supplied under our Deemed Contract Rates which may not be the best option for your business. You may be better off signing a fixed price contract instead. If you'd like to find out more information about the details in this letter or a fixed price contract, please go online to: www.cbfenergy.com/sme-pricechange. Thank you for being an CBF Energy customer."

My interpretation of this paragraph is as follows:

"You are currently supplied under our Deemed Contract Rate which may not be the best option for your business. We in fact know what is the best option for your business but we're not really interested in telling you, because we make more money out of you that way. You can go and visit our website to find out what is the best arrangement for you, but that will almost certainly be too much effort and we hope therefore that this letter will end up in the bin and we can carry on overcharging you for your electricity".

"Sorry, smile's off..."

C... is for Copying Someone Else's Ideas

What's wrong with that!?! More fortunes have been made from copying someone else's ideas than from coming up with new ones that's for sure.

Heather could be learning new processes and techniques from other hairdressers, Gary could be copying advertising and marketing methods from other gas engineers in his locality. None of your competitors will have a legal right to protect any of these things and you should not feel any sense of shame in blatantly copying what they do, particularly if they are successful at it. You may even take some of those methods and processes and develop them further.

It is one of the commonly held misconceptions that in order to have a successful business you have to come up with an original idea. Nothing could be further from the truth.

You should always be very aware of what your competition is doing as it will all happen silently in the background. No-one is going to knock on your door and say "By the way have you heard what such and such a company up the road is doing". You have to be out there researching this fact, either by talking to customers of the competition, or if possible visiting their places of business or even calling them up.

C... is for Competitors

Be nice to your competitors when you meet them and at all times be polite to them. When you get the opportunity to do so engage them in friendly conversation, as this is a great opportunity to find out what they're up to. Networking groups are ideal for this, particularly the ones in the evening where a little judicious use of alcoholic beverages can serve to loosen tongues. In fact alcohol plus a sprinkling of flattery is a tactic that rarely fails when it comes to a bit of tongue loosening.
Never, ever bad mouth your competition. This will almost certainly come back to bite you later. Remember, what goes around, comes around.

D... is for Delivery

Delivery, delivery, delivery has got to be your absolute maxim at all times. You will build a business by delivering quality products and services. You can forget everything that you've ever learnt about marketing because when it comes to delivery this is the one thing above all else that's going to grow your business. If you can find a way of doing it more cheaply for customers, quicker for customers or in a way that is better than the competition then your business will prosper.

"You'll have to forgive my wife... this is the longest she's ever been on a diet"

D... is for Determination

Determination is the single most important attribute for success in business. The good news is that you can develop a determined state of mind. In other words this is not something you have to be born with. Forget intelligence, looks, charm, luck, this is the single most important characteristic you will need to succeed. Remember... where there's a will, there's a way.

D... is for Deal

Enthusiasm is the enemy of a bargain. A very useful phrase to help you remember how to get the best from a deal, especially when you are in the role of the purchaser.

The sales person sitting opposite you wants to hear the magic word 'yes', as in yes I will buy that product at the price that you have just specified. What he doesn't want to hear, particularly after he's spent a good half an hour, talking to you and hearing all your warm words of encouragement is... "Well thank you very much for that splendid presentation, and I'll get back to you if I need anything further" because what the sales person believes he is hearing when you say that is... 'thanks but no thanks'. So as you stand up and walk away from the table this is the point when you MAY hear the magic words "There is a chance I can do something with that price...".

What you don't know about the sales person is where they are in their monthly sales targets. As you are sitting there chirruping your warm words of encouragement, the sales person may well have been thinking "Thank God for that, at least I'll be able to fill my quota for the month", and of course if that was indeed the case you have an excellent opportunity to secure yourself a good deal. Be prepared to walk away, walking away is good.

D... is for Delegation

There are two very important things you need to know about delegation. Firstly, you will never grow a large business if you cannot delegate and secondly delegation is not abdication.

There is only one of you and your time is finite. As your business grows and you become more successful you will need to develop ways of rationing out that time to the greatest benefit. You cannot be everywhere at once and you will need to pass some tasks down to your staff. Letting go of these tasks is always difficult as no one is ever going to feel as passionate about your business as you do.
Be that as it may, letting go is what you will need to do.

Having passed on the task it doesn't mean that you've passed on overall responsibility. If that member of staff messes up that task you are ultimately still responsible for it. You must learn how to monitor performance of the task that you have passed on and perish the thought that something should go wrong, you must act quickly to remedy matters. It is like being in a helicopter. You can ride around above everything that's going on below you, but are also able to survey it and swoop down to the ground if there is anything below you that attracts your attention. It will take a while to develop that alertness to know what needs swooping down on and what to ignore.

E... is for Equity

Equity in a business is what you have invested in it. In other words your share capital. One thing you should know about this is that you should never give it away. You may be tempted with the success of your business to reward your employees with a share-ownership – do not do this. Your employees should be rewarded with bonuses and salary. Remember they haven't taken the risk that you've taken to set up this business. Your reward is in the value of the growing business and the dividends you get from it. Do not confuse rewards of risk with the rewards of performance.

E... is for Excellence

If it isn't going to be excellent... why bother?

I recently read a book by a so called business guru and one of his mantras was that 'good is good enough', and further, he reckoned that excellence was overrated.

Suffice to say, I disagree.

Chris has also read this book and he's decided that he is going to build his business on 'good is good enough'. He pitches up at his client's offices to install some software into their PCs, at 9.08 am. He was actually booked to arrive at 9.00 am but well, you know the traffic and everything, and it's nearly 9.00 am so it's not such a big deal so 9.08 am well, that's good enough. Chris looks like an unmade bed at the best of times, but on this particular day he is wearing yesterday's shirt.

A quick sniff test at 8.30 am as he's rushing out the door indicated to him that this shirt was going to be definitely good enough. I mean it's not as if he's Ralph Lauren! He's paid to fix PCs, he's not paid to be a clothes horse! Chris sets about his work with his usual gusto, and roundabout 11.00 am he is close to completing his task. It's been a warmer than expected day and yesterday's shirt is starting to let Chris down a little. He figures he is going to be ok as long as no-one comes near him and reckons about a 2 yard radius from his desk is going to suffice. He is normally quite a chatty bloke but on this occasion he's decided that a policy of scowling will keep people away from that 2 metre total exclusion zone. Chris rapidly finishes off his task and exits the door without bothering to say goodbye to anyone. As far as he's concerned he's paid to fix PCs he's not paid for small talk and in any event it will be cheaper for them in the long run. He's head down and no chatter.

Will Chris, or smelly Chris as he's now referred to by the client, be invited back for more work? I don't think so.

Aim for excellence, you may not always achieve it, but how could you possibly aim any lower?

F... is for Failure

If success is the last stop on the journey, then failure is going to be one of the stops along the way. You will not find any successful businessman that has not suffered his fair share of failure along the road to success. If any of their flashy autobiographies are worth reading, they are worth doing so to find out how these people coped with failure. The mental sturdiness required to get over failure is one of the things that separates successful people from unsuccessful people. In just coping with that failure and carrying on you are already proving yourself to be of greater merit than average.

The most important aspect to failure is, of course, to learn from it. It is, I think, worth documenting after a major failure exactly how it happened. Painful though this is, the actual writing out of the episode will help to ensure that the same mistake is not going to happen again. A simple A4 page statement should include the following:

- The circumstances surrounding the failed event (e.g. public speaking engagement, e-mail marketing campaign, product demonstration, new hair treatment);

- An analysis of exactly what aspect of the event actually failed; and

- How this failure can be avoided in the future.

Writing all of this down will bring a sense of closure to the event itself. With closure there is a sense of moving on.

F... is for Firing

Once you become an employer it's sadly true that as night follows day you will one day also become a firer. Employment decisions don't always work out. It may be the employee's fault, it may be your fault, it may be to do with a number of reasons, but the reality is once it starts going wrong you must end it and you must end it quickly and lawfully. To not end it is not good for you, not good for your business and also, very importantly, it's not good for the employee either. The chances are that they are not the lazy, feckless, idiot that you think they are, they are just in the wrong job!

The law on sacking people, broadly, is that provided the reason has nothing to do with age, race, sex or any other form of discrimination you can fire someone for poor performance or conduct any time within the first one year without having to go through the full due process of written warnings (this law is under consideration to change to two years). Having said that, you need also to be fair to the employee and set a standard for yourself, so at least one warning with time after to improve would be the minimum that would be reasonable.

What you must be, however, is decisive, concise and honest. You must also tell the employee face to face what is going to happen to them and the reasons for you doing it. It will be painful for you, it will be painful for them, but the sooner it's over the better.

F... is for Fear

Another negative word so I've decided to put both negative words all on the same page so that we can get through this quickly. Fear is natural and fear can be a motivator. Fear produces in us adrenalin enabling us to run quicker, think smarter and in other words it's a force for action. Owning your own business means that you will experience much more extremes of emotion than you ever did as an employee. When the downs come they are really downs. Being on your own means that quite often you have no-one to talk to and confide in.

No matter how bad it looks, it almost certainly isn't as bad as you think. Fear is usually a fear of the unknown and not of the known. Fear is what you think might happen, what you think might be on the horizon, not what is actually all around you. Take stock of your fears, analyse them, lay them out in front of you on a virtual table. Imagine picking each one up in turn and asking yourself what actually are the possibilities of this happening. As you go through each of these items on the table, you will realise that taken in turn the chances of your worst fears being realised is extremely small. Don't give fear the chance to manifest itself into panic.

Be good to yourself and do all the obviously good things for your mental and physical health. It is true what your granny told you and drinking too much, eating too much, not sleeping enough and not doing enough exercise is a great way of

"I don't think I could have picked a tougher line of work"

developing a successful breeding ground for fear. Also...don't read the newspapers and don't watch the news. This may seem a little drastic, but it has been proved in empirical tests that if you are already feeling down, seeing the news is not going to make you feel any better. Journalists are trained that bad news sells newspapers, and for the most part your daily news bulletin or your daily newspaper is going to contain mostly bad news. If you're feeling down about your business you've got quite enough bad news to be going on with without taking on the problems of the World as well.

Remember tough times don't last, tough people do.

F... is for Frugality

Five star hotels and fancy cars will have to wait (not too long we hope!). For the time being frugality is the watch word. For most of the four characters this will generally mean being careful about personal expenditure, particularly during the first year. A good rule of thumb is to work out the absolute minimum you need to get by for the first year and make sure you stick to it. Remember what you're aiming for is a healthy cash balance at the end of the first year. Cash is King.

F... is for Follow Up

One of the biggest mistakes small businesses make once they've seen a potential prospect is to not follow up. This is not at all relevant to Heather, but as we will talk about later she needs to keep in touch with the customers that she serves. This needs to be a light touch. Gary will definitely need to follow up on any meetings he's had with prospective customers, particularly where they are commercial customers. If Chris has a meeting with a potential client, it will quite often be in the form of a site survey. The potential client will talk to him about their network and their PCs which will enable Chris to write back to them as a follow up and recommend any improvements that he deems necessary.

As we will later learn, Simon will be meeting the prospects and explaining a product to them that will be an entirely new concept. It is therefore vital that Simon follows up that meeting within a week to ask the prospect if they've had time to consider the proposal, and particularly whether they have any questions regarding the product's implementation, ease of use and most of all, pricing.

G... is for Giving Up

As Churchill once said 'Never, Ever, Ever, Give Up'.

G... is for Goals

You must have a goal, in fact you must have many goals. Many smaller goals build up to achieving the bigger goal. Without goals the prospects are that you will drift along aimlessly hoping for the best. The goals could be as simple as, say, to build a web-site by such and such a date, attend such and such an exhibition, sign-up for such and such a networking group. All of these goals are realistic and achievable. What is not realistic and achievable is to set yourself vague goals about the amount of money you are going to generate in your first year. The reality is that you have no real control over that but you do have control over the smaller goals that lead up to generating that income. Setting unrealistic goals is a sure fire way of ensuring your enthusiasm hits the buffers. Set down all your first year goals and put a time-line against them. Make sure you stick to the time-line.

G... is for Getting Rich Quick

You have probably seen some of the adverts, which go something like this:

"Twelve months ago I was emptying bins for Salford Council, and now I own a 50 acre estate with a small fleet of Lamborghinis and spend my evenings drinking fine wines! and you could too...

... by following my simple 24 step programme. All yours for just £9.99" (or something similar).

Surprise, surprise there are no shortcuts to getting rich, or even slightly rich. Do not be tempted by the shortcuts. Remember the only way to get rich from a get rich quick book, is to write one!

G... is for Google Ad Words (or Pay Per Click)

If you were to go onto Google and search for a business in your local area, for example, plumbers in Teddington, there will be a list of local plumbers along with names of listing organisations containing local plumbers. Right at the very top of the first page and along the far right hand column there will be ads that have been paid for using Google Ad Words. The other results will have been generated purely internally and are listed by popularity. If Gary wants to ensure that when someone needs a gas engineer in his area they find him first, he can pay for this privilege on Google Ad Words.

The way it works is that he only pays when someone clicks on that ad and he can bid to be anywhere he wants on the listing, be it first, second, third, fourth page, etc. Gary may be unlucky in that he is one of 100 people wanting to do the same thing and therefore if he wishes to ensure a high listing, he may have to bid quite a bit of money. Gary can be clever about how he uses Google Ad Words in that providing he specifies his location exactly, and at what time of the day he wants his ad to appear, he can limit his cost. There are two really good things about Google Ad Words, firstly, you can very much control your cost and secondly, it is mostly done on-line and it is very easy to use. The bad things about Google Ad Words are if you can't follow the instructions on the web-site they are virtually impossible to get through to on the phone.

This form of advertising is extremely useful for someone like Gary, some use to someone like Chris, but of almost no use to Simon and very little use to Heather. Gary would be well served to make a considerable investment in this kind of advertising as it is slowly but surely taking the place of Yellow Pages.

G... is for Google Places

Google Places is a completely free service and can be signed up for in very little time. If you are signed up for Google Places, what will happen is that if someone Googles your company name a little map will appear on the Google search page showing exactly where you are, along with possibly a photograph or two and if you wish a video of your organisation. This enables you to give a much fuller description of yourself should someone be searching for you, and best of all it is completely free!

G... is for Group On

At the time of writing, group on is a major marketing tool used in the United States which is just beginning to take off in the United Kingdom. Simply, this is a scheme whereby discounts can be obtained by buying in bulk. If enough subscribers to group on are interested in a particular product or service it can help drive down the price in a given location. Both Gary and Heather should consider putting their services forward through group on as it could help generate new customers. For more information go to www.groupon.co.uk

H... is for Health and Holidays

One thing you are going to need in abundance to make this business a success is stamina, and you will not have stamina if you are in poor health. Self-employed people take less sick days than employed people and take less risks with their health. The days when you would quite happily spend six hours on the town getting hammered, getting a taxi home at 3.00am in the morning, followed by four hours sleep resulting in a call to the office at 9.00am "sorry chaps I'm not able to make it in today"...

Well they are long gone.

Self-employed people are the ones that you will see quietly creeping out the door before midnight to make sure they get their full 8 hours of sleep before the day ahead.

Your annual 28 days holiday (28 includes Bank Holidays) are also sadly now a thing of the past. That's not to say that you will not be rewarded in the future with lots of lovely holidays, but for now and possibly the next three or four years, a snatched week in somewhere hopefully sunny with your Blackberry firmly strapped to your side is about the best you can expect.

H... is for HMRC

Tax needn't be taxing... or so the advert will have us believe. It will certainly be taxing if you make the simple mistake of calling HMRC. Trying to talk to HMRC is like nailing jelly to a wall. It is difficult, often painful and ultimately futile.

My advice is to get your accountant to do it! It is one of the things they are paid to do. So, if you do have an accountant, DO NOT IN ANY CIRCUMSTANCES call HMRC.

You must at all times remember that HMRC is the organisation that is tasked by the Government to raise money for the Government to spend. HMRC is not an organisation that exists to help you, the tax payer. It exists to help the Government, the tax spender. This doesn't make them bad people, it's just that they want your money, and they want as much of your money as they can get their hands on – so trust your accountant to make sure this doesn't happen.

I

I… is for If

If you wish to read something every day that is going to inspire you then you can do no worse than Rudyard Kipling's 'IF'. He talks about many things in this poem but the one line that I think of every, single day is the one about filling the unforgiving minute. Remember our greatest enemy is time. Read this poem, it is a classic.

IF

IF you can keep your head when all about you
Are losing theirs and blaming it on you,
If you can trust yourself when all men doubt you,
But make allowance for their doubting too;
If you can wait and not be tired by waiting,
Or being lied about, don't deal in lies,
Or being hated, don't give way to hating,
And yet don't look too good, nor talk too wise:
If you can dream - and not make dreams your master;
If you can think - and not make thoughts your aim;
If you can meet with Triumph and Disaster
And treat those two impostors just the same;
If you can bear to hear the truth you've spoken
Twisted by knaves to make a trap for fools,
Or watch the things you gave your life to, broken,
And stoop and build 'em up with worn-out tools:

If you can make one heap of all your winnings
And risk it on one turn of pitch-and-toss,
And lose, and start again at your beginnings
And never breathe a word about your loss;
If you can force your heart and nerve and sinew
To serve your turn long after they are gone,
And so hold on when there is nothing in you
Except the Will which says to them: 'Hold on!'
If you can talk with crowds and keep your virtue,
' Or walk with Kings - nor lose the common touch,
if neither foes nor loving friends can hurt you,
If all men count with you, but none too much;
If you can fill the unforgiving minute
With sixty seconds' worth of distance run,
Yours is the Earth and everything that's in it,
And - which is more - you'll be a Man, my son! (...or daughter!)

I... is for Income Tax

A subject dear to my heart! Income tax is the tax payable on the profits of your business. This will be in the form of corporation tax if you have formed a limited company. What you must be aware of when it comes to the matter of income tax is that tax is only payable on profits. If you have made a loss you won't pay tax. Tax is a percentage of that profit and for small businesses that rate starts at 20%. So in very obvious terms if you've made sales of £100 and you have costs of £40 it means you've made a profit of £60. The tax you will therefore pay on that is 20% of £60, i.e. £12.

There is a common mistaken belief that you can spend your way out of a tax bill. I've heard many clients say "Well I'd rather pay £12 to buy some more equipment than pay £12 to the tax man". If you think about the maths that simply does not work. If an extra £12 was to be spent that would mean the costs being not £40 but £52 and what happens is that the tax bill goes down by just 20% of £12 i.e. the tax goes down by £2.40 to £9.60 **it does not go down by £12.**

Income tax is a good thing! Income tax is what keeps the Country going and without it we would all be in lots and lots of trouble so don't be afraid of paying income tax, be proud of paying income tax. Clearly, you will wish to pay much less tax than you were as an employee and clearly you will wish to take advantage of every legal route available to do so, but be aware of one thing, the more tax you are paying the more profits you are making.

Do you want to make profits or do you want to make losses?

I... is for Interviewing New Employees

A common mistake that people make when interviewing new employees is to talk at the candidate about their business and about the prospects of working in it, while the candidate just sits there nodding appreciatively.

After about ten minutes of this the interviewee is asked if he's got any questions. the questions are asked in due course, answered by the interviewer and the candidate is promptly offered the job. In all of that time the interviewer has learnt precisely nothing about the interviewee.

A useful acronym is WASP, which stands for Welcome, Acquire, Supply, Part. All four parts of this are important. Welcome the candidate with a strong handshake and a smile, relax the candidate, acquire information from the candidate about their reasons for wanting this job and ask them several questions derived from their CV. Asking pre-prepared standard questions to all candidates is good practice and gives a basis for comparison. Once that has been done then you can supply information about the job itself and your business and by that time you will know whether the information you are supplying matches with the information they have supplied. If there isn't a match then the conversation thereafter should be brief!

Finally, parting is also important, do not at that stage tell them that they've got the job but say that you will be thinking about it and be getting in touch with them or their agent in the very near future.

I... is for Investment Capital

Investment capital is what you are going to need to set up the business and to survive on whilst the business is generating cash. The latter is known as working capital. How much you need will obviously depend on the kind of business you are going to set up. Heather the hairdresser is going to need to put a deposit down on the lease of her shop, she is going to need to fit out that shop and all of this is going to be quite expensive. It is imperative that all these facts and figures are known before she starts, and they are relatively easy to obtain. The local estate agent can provide costs for rent and business rates for shops along the high street and a quick search on Google will enable her to find shop-fitters who can quote for the fitting out. Heather will already be aware of the equipment that she will need to get started and will probably know the suppliers that can give her costs for this equipment. If at all possible this equipment should be obtained as very good quality second-hand equipment rather than brand new equipment.

For Gary and Chris the start-up costs are a lot lower and consist mainly of working capital. Both of them would have had experience of how to price their services and how much revenue they generated whilst they were with their former employers. Both of them will need to have a web-site designed (see W for web-site) and they should factor in the cost of that along with any equipment they may need that they don't already own. The bigger unknown for both of them is how much revenue they are going to generate, particularly in their first year. I would say a good rule of thumb is that in their first year they will generate half the revenue for their businesses that they generated for their former employers. Working backwards from that figure and already knowing what they need to live on, they will be able to work out how much investment capital they need.

I've already mentioned banks and using them as an avenue for raising finance, but by far the better avenue is to raise it from your own funds. This means planning from a long way out and saving up the money that you need. I know it is an old-fashioned notion to save money, but it is going to be a much cheaper and less frightening prospect than borrowing it from a financial institution. The other alternative is, of course, to borrow from friends and family, (who will hopefully be a little bit more flexible on the loan repayments!) What is most important is that you don't run out of cash, because running out of cash is where you start to make poor decisions. If you budget on your business being slow to build at the beginning and fund yourself accordingly, you will undoubtedly be more relaxed as the year goes on.

With Simon the situation is completely different as he is really in the great unknown. If his software takes off he is likely to be extremely successful and this is because the cost of delivering software is very low compared to the price at which the software is sold. On the other hand, if he doesn't sell any... things get a bit stickier. One thing I think he ought to do is to budget on making zero sales in his first year. I will go into more detail as to why this may be in his particular business in the section on marketing. Simon's start up costs are also going to be quite high, and that is why he is in the riskiest of the four businesses. He will need to make a heavy investment in marketing during that first year so in short, his budget ought to be zero sales, lots of marketing costs, plus his own living costs and this should determine how much capital he will need.

I... is for IR35

IR35 is a piece of tax legislation that is something taken extremely seriously by contractors (particularly IT contractors) and is virtually completely unknown by the rest of the population. IT contractors in particular need to be aware of the implications of IR35.

This piece of legislation is there principally to protect HMRC from disguised employment. This is particularly true of individuals who are turning up at the same place of work day in, day out, being supervised by a line manager and at the same time operating as if they owned a business. HMRC regards this as disguised employment and will seek to have that individual taxed as if they were so. Being taxed as an employee is going to be much more expensive than the tax implications of owning your own business.

None of our four individuals are in this situation and need not worry about this particular piece of legislation. All of them have multiple income streams and none of which in any way could be regarded as disguised employment.

J

J… is for Job

You don't have one!

Remember you own a business, so think like a business owner, not like an employee. An employee can always blame someone else if things go wrong. The software wasn't right, the boss gave me the wrong instructions, the customer's an idiot, etc, etc, etc. You're a business owner and if anything goes wrong you've got no-one else to blame but yourself. You can't even blame your staff – remember they work for you!

J… is for Jags

Okay so you've had your first two years, you've survived and further to that you are actually prospering!

Time for a new car…

Well, why not? Success deserves reward. But before you go rushing down to the new car showroom, a cautionary tale involving two clients of mine.

A Tale of Two Jags

Some years ago a client of mine, for reasons best known to himself, decided that he wanted a brand new Jaguar sports car. He couldn't afford to buy one outright, so for a couple of thousand pound down, a £750 per month hire purchase payment and a balloon payment of £20,000 after three years, he got himself his brand new Jaguar. Surprise, surprise this client could not make the £20,000 balloon payment after three years, consequently had to refinance, and eight years after he took delivery of the car, he's still paying for it.

Another client of mine, who on any given day could afford to buy a brand new Jaguar sports car several times over out of the cash in his bank, also decided one day that he wanted such a car. He chose to buy a three year old Jaguar that cost him £25K. Intrigued I asked him why he didn't buy a brand new one, as he could clearly afford to do so. His reply was very revealing. He said "I can't see myself ever being rich enough to be that stupid". A little harsh said I, and he further explained "Well, the car had done 15,000 miles from new which is approximately 10% of its working life and cost me half of the list price". So as the Americans say 'do the maths' – You can't argue with the logic.

J... is for Jargon

When you were back in the corporate world you made it your business to learn all the jargon. You knew all about downsizing, leverage, benchmarking and re-engineering. You were exceptionally clued up as to how empowerment was going to propel you up the greasy pole.

Fun though it is to laugh at corporate world jargon, it does serve its purpose in that particular world. It is a way of making sure that you can identify people of the same tribe, or indeed people that are singing off the same hymn sheet, to use another piece of jargon.

Well that world is now long behind you and now you have to explain things in a simple and effective way.

Gary, who knew his last firm's mission statement off by heart, is determined to develop his own one man mission statement. 70 year old Mrs Jones (whose boiler Gary will be fixing today) thinks that Gary's mission statement should be 'Fix that Boiler'. Or to be more precise, 'Fix that boiler, don't take too long about it, don't leave a mess, and charge me a reasonable price'.

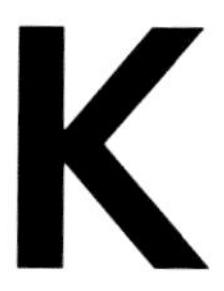

K… is for Kings

There are two kings in business that you must, (if it's not too strong a word) worship. The first is the customer and the second is cash.

You must know everything there is to know about your customer. You must know what your likely customer is going to look like, where they are going to be buying your products and services, what they are looking for when they choose those products and services and how much they are prepared to pay for those products and services. You must also know what they are likely to complain about if things go wrong and more importantly how you are going to get them to recommend you to other people. You must know your customer inside out. For Heather the hairdresser, it is a relatively simple process. The majority, but not all of her customers, are going to be female, they are going to buy her services when they need their hair cut, dried or styled. The price they are willing to pay for that will be judged by what else is available on that particular town's high street and, of course… every woman knows what a hair disaster looks like!

Cash, or the lack of it, is the reason why most businesses fail. It is not necessarily because they don't have enough sales, or prospects of sales, it's simply that they run out of money. Money in the bank, Frank, is what ensures a good night's sleep. Having money left over in the bank is, of course, a consequence of two things. What is coming in and what is going out! That is stating the obvious but you need to control both of those aspects if a nice, healthy balance is going to remain in the account. For Heather and Gary cash coming in happens at the delivery of the service, so providing there are enough people buying the services, they are in a much better position to control cash than Simon and Chris.

Simon and Chris will be issuing invoices for their work and products and will be looking for their customers to pay up those invoices within 14 to 30 days. Between 30 and 45 days is the accepted industry standard. Asking for money is something all of us find difficult, but it is something that must be done. If you have delivered a quality service and 45 days has gone past and your customer hasn't paid, you need to ask them for the money. You need to do this in a polite way, but you need to be persistent. It may well be that you have to ask several times before the money comes up. Be sure that you are polite on every occasion but build yourself a programme whereby you are asking for the money at regular intervals. E-mail is almost certainly the best way of doing this, although some people will say that nothing can beat a phone conversation. The problem with a phone conversation is that the person on the other end of the line could well be your direct contact and you don't want to get into any embarrassing conversations! That's why e-mail is the best because in the good old British way we can pretend it's all not happening. An example of a debt chasing e-mail is as follows:

> Hope you are well.
> Could you please check the following outstanding invoices that I have on my records:
>
> **Invoice No 4332 for £88.13 dated 31/10/2008; and**
> **Invoice No.6050 for £176.25 dated 26/1/2010.**
>
> Both invoices relate to the preparation of your tax returns (Let me know if you need copies of these invoices).
> If you agree they are outstanding please pay as soon as possible by cheque or direct to:
>
> Natwest
> Account number: 12345678
> Sort code: 12-23-34
>
> Regards

If your customer is a large organisation, it always helps to understand how the payment authorisation process works. Your direct contact who originally hired you will not be the individual that is raising the cheque or organising the payment directly into your bank account. That individual will almost certainly be part of the authorisation process but not part of the actual paying process. The paying process will be organised by a person in the accounts department responsible for the bought ledger. You could do a lot worse than to get to know this person and there is no harm at all in introducing yourself to this person by phone once you have issued your first invoice. It could be a very simple call just to enquire as to whether your invoice has arrived and who it is that you are speaking to. If after 45 days your invoice hasn't been paid then this is the person that you could politely call to find out what the issues are.

Of course you will run into situations where despite all your politeness you still have not got the money. My suggestion is that if the client has not paid you after three reminders (and the debt is now over 60 days old), you should issue a final warning saying that legal action will commence if payment is not forthcoming. You might think this is all a bit heavy and frightening and will cost you thousands and thousands of pounds in lawyers' fees, but the reality is most debt disputes can be solved in the Small Claims Court and a County Court Summons can be issued from as little as £75. The good news is also that lawyers need not be involved!

L

L... is for Limited Company

Should your new venture be a Limited company or a sole trader? A limited company is one in which the liability of the shareholder is literally limited to the amount that the shareholder has invested. The minimum amount that a shareholder can invest is £1. A limited company can be set up with just one share of £1 and one director. The limited company bit is important because if the company goes bust it means that you don't go bust with it i.e your personal assets are ring fenced and protected from creditors. Over the years this little piece of company law has been abused by many people, and you should be careful not to fall into that particular trap.

The alternative to a limited company is trading as a sole trader but should things go pear shaped all of your assets are at risk.

For me, therefore, this particular element is the chief reason why I recommend people to form limited companies rather than sole trader businesses. The down side to being limited is that you are plugged in a little bit deeper into the Government system and your accountancy bills are likely to be slightly higher than they would be if you were a sole trader. The other chief benefit at the time of writing is that generally speaking you would pay less tax within the limited company than you would as a sole trader.

Forming a limited company is these days actually easier than setting up a bank account. There is a plethora of companies throughout the United Kingdom who will form limited companies for sometimes even less than £50. There is a potential sting in the tail however, as these companies often charge £150 a year thereafter to perform relatively simple tasks like filing your annual return. As ever, be aware of the small print!

L... is for Luck

An old blues singer once said, when talking about luck, 'if it wasn't for bad luck I'd have no luck at all'.

Some people will tell you that the great business people would not have got their massive fortunes without a very healthy dose of luck and being in the right place at the right time. The reality is that most people will have good luck and bad luck in equal measures. You could win the lottery tomorrow, or be knocked down by a bus tomorrow, but the chances of either of these things happening are absolutely miniscule. For most of us it is all about playing the hand that we are dealt. The difference between a good businessman and a bad businessman is that the good businessman capitalises on that luck with great speed, and the bad businessman prevaricates. The good businessman acknowledges when his

luck has turned against him, and makes rapid decisions to alleviate the problems caused by that bad luck. The bad businessman wallows in his misfortune and blames the world.

As for being in the right place at the right time, the right place is here and the right time is now - and that has always been the case.

It is marginally true that the best time to start a business is in a recession and not in a boom. When looked at over a long period of time though, it is of no consequence at what point the business is started.

L... is for Location

Location, location, location is the mantra of the retailer. For Simon, Gary and Chris, location is not of any great significance, and it is certainly not worth spending a lot of money trying to get this particular bit of the business plan correct.

For Heather of course it is absolutely vital.

It is questionable whether Heather will want to set up a new shop in a town where competition is already fierce. Ideally she will want to set up in a town where there aren't too many hairdressers already in existence.

With the internet at everybody's fingertips, it is relatively easy to do the research on what is known as 'The demographics'. A simple question put in to Google such as 'How many people live in X town' will reveal a breakdown of the number of people in that town by gender and age. Walking down the town's high street is probably the best way of finding out how many competing hairdressers there are, and a quick visit to the local estate agent will tell you how much the rents are on that street. Heather can find out for herself how much the potential competition is charging for their services. Having gathered all of that information she is able to compare towns in her area. What she will be looking for is a judicious combination of all those factors, ideally a town where rents are relatively low. She will be looking for a town where rents are relatively low in comparison to the prices charged, and the number of hairdressers is relatively low in comparison to the number of females living in the town.

Heather may also consider obtaining some market research data from the likes of Keynote, Mintel, etc. These organisations have written in-depth market research reports on all manner of industries and copies of the reports can be obtained for a relatively small amount of money. For the price of a return ticket into London, Heather may also consider going to the British Library where much of this information can be obtained free of charge.

L... is for Linked In

Linked in is sometimes known as 'Professionals Facebook'. It works very much along similar lines to Facebook and it certainly proved particularly useful for people who are either looking to hire someone or people who are looking to get their CV out to potential hirers. None of this is, of course, of any interest to our four characters but what Linked In is also very good at is discussion forums. There are very many discussion groups on Linked In that cover all manner of topics, but would certainly include topics that could be either of use as a reader to Simon and Gary and also an opportunity for both of them to advertise their services.

Linked In would be exceptionally good for the likes of Chris as it would enable him to join many forums dealing with the ever complicated nature of his business. This is not so much to advertise his business but to keep abreast of all the developments in this sector.

M... is for Marketing

Acres and acres of perfectly good woodland have been sacrificed in the production of books on marketing. It would probably take you a lifetime to read all of them and it's questionable whether you would know anymore about the subject than you do right this minute.

So what is marketing? In very simple terms marketing is putting your products or services in front of the potential customer. The key questions therefore are "Where is the market, who is going to be in the market place and how am I going to persuade the customer to part with their hard earned cash to buy my product or service?"

This is a huge topic and also more than that it is possibly the most important topic for anybody setting up their business. What we are going to do therefore is to look at each of the four characters and the different marketing challenges facing each of them.

Heather's Marketing

So starting with Heather, her market is almost certainly no more than a two mile radius from where her shop is and her customers are basically anybody who has hair. There is no point Heather advertising in Lincoln if her shop is in Brighton, so in very simplistic terms Heather's marketing efforts must be local.

Heather's principal advertising is the very fact that she's on the high street, and therefore it's imperative that everything about Heather's shop is well designed and built. Heather's shop will almost certainly not be the only hairdressing shop on the high street and therefore it is probably worth her making a big noise at the very beginning to get people into the shop in the first place. She's confident in her own abilities and is very excited about some new innovations and methods that she believes her competitors are not capable of. In the long run, advertising is going to be of limited use to Heather, as she is going to be relying on repeat business from customers and also from referrals she will get from happy customers. The key therefore is to get people into the shop in the first place and to do that she may well consider advertising in the local press and also offering substantial discounts to first time customers. It is worth making these discounts substantial, for example 50% off, because people tend to have loyalty to their hairdresser and will require serious persuading to get them to try something else.

The great thing about Heather's business is that it involves built in recurrence. Heather knows with absolute certainty that her customers' hair will carry on growing! This means that they are going to have to come back in six to eight weeks to have the whole process done again. Clearly, it is important therefore to grab the customer at the point of sale and persuade them to come back to the same place in six to eight weeks. Clearly, six weeks is better than eight and the customer could be incentivised to make that appointment there and then, if say a 10 or 15% discount was given. The customer's mobile and e-mail address should be requested so that they can be reminded of their appointment. The other key aspect of this is of course, data capture to build up the database. Heather will need to ensure that she keeps building that customer's database so that she can market directly to them at a later date. Heather's business is likely to be the most busy at weekends and the least busy in the daytime during the week. It is obviously sensible therefore to structure her pricing accordingly. Customers could be incentivised to come at quieter times of the week and in so doing benefit from discounts. Similarly, Christmas time is the busiest time and January is the quietest time. Heather should use her database to heavily discount processes and treatments during the month of January to entice customers in during the quieter times.

Heather will need to buy a programme that automatically sends out the texts and email addresses for the reminders, and there are many of these programmes on the market. I doubt if there is any point in sending successive marketing messages to customers who are regulars, but it will certainly be important to keep in touch with those customers who are occasional visitors. If someone is planning to get their haircut in any particular week and is undecided as to where they are going to go, a timely message from Heather offering a 10% discount could be a deciding factor.

Gary's Marketing

Gary is in a similar situation but that mile radius could be pushed out to anything up to 10 miles, but probably no more than that. Gary's customers are anybody who has the responsibility of paying for a central heating system, or the installation of a central heating system (building contractors). The latter is important as Gary might pick up work from building contractors that might take him further afield than ten miles.

Once Gary has fixed his customer's boiler hopefully they won't call him again for a long time. Gary's customers only need Gary when something catastrophic has happened. Gary's customers will therefore wish to see the back of Gary in the nicest possible way, as they hope Gary's repairs will prove long lasting. Gary must therefore ensure that his name comes to peoples' minds when the catastrophic event happens. This is not an easy task.

In the old days before networking and the internet, gas engineers would take out large adverts in Yellow Pages and Thompsons and other local directories and this would form their principal advertising. When the householders' boiler went down the cry would go up "Where's the Yellow Pages!" They would leaf through the yellow door stop obtain four or five numbers, get some competitive quotes and make a decision on who they were going to call.

It is also possible that this person may know someone who could recommend an engineer. It is possible that one of their neighbours had experienced a similar event recently and they might call them and say "did such and such do a good job for you? If so do you have their number".

Much of that marketing process is unchanged, but the internet has largely taken the place of the Yellow Pages. I say largely, because it has not completely meant the death of the Yellow Pages. It is likely that many people under the age of 40 won't even know what the Yellow Pages are. Familiarity with the internet for people between the ages of 50 and 60 is patchy, and between the ages of 60 and 70 extremely patchy. 70 year old Mrs Jones has heard of the internet, and wants nothing to do with it. She has used the Yellow Pages for years and will carry on doing so, and Gary should be aware of this fact. The price for advertising in the Yellow Pages has decreased markedly and so has the number of competitors listed in the Yellow Pages. It will be some decades before the Yellow Pages disappears altogether and Gary should be mindful of that.

Twenty years ago networking groups hardly existed outside the Chamber of Commerce, and now they have proliferated everywhere. Gary should sign himself up for as many networking groups as he can. Not all will prove useful to him, and over time he will probably settle on three or four groups that he visits on a regular basis. If he's in a breakfast meeting of 40 people in the middle of Winter and that morning someone's boiler breaks down, he is in an excellent position of getting that business. He will also have the opportunity to make contacts with building contractors who could offer him longer term and more substantial, commercial work.

Most of Gary's new business is probably going to be generated by advertising through the internet. He will also wish to consider becoming a member of local internet advertising groups. One such group is called 'The Best of Group' which has achieved great success over the last five years. This is a relatively cheap way of advertising your services on what is essentially someone else's web-site.

Later on I will be talking about web-sites and search engine optimisation, both of which are going to be pretty important to Gary. Gary may also wish to consider pay per click or Google Ad Words. (See G for Google Ad Words). Once Gary has completed his work at the customer's premises he must make sure that the customer is left with plenty of easy ways of obtaining Gary's number should they need to. This will be more than just a "do not hesitate to contact me Madam should anything go wrong", but is a way of making sure the customer can get access to Gary's number quickly should they be asked by someone else. All central heating apparatus is kept away in cupboards somewhere in the house. Gary should be smart and make sure he has a large sticker that he can put on the inside of that cupboard somewhere prominent. Gary should tell the customer that he has done this before he leaves the customer's premises. He should also leave several business cards and also, ask the customer to make a note in their address book, (paper or phone) so that it will be easy to find.

Branding is also going to be quite important to Gary. His van should be branded very clearly with his business name and number. Gary should make sure that he avoids any of the pointless slogans that some tradesmen are tempted to put on the side of their vehicles – "You've tried the rest now try the best" etc, etc, etc and other such nonsense. The best example of branding I have ever seen was actually done by a client of mine who is a pest controller. He has a high sided vehicle and on both sides of it is a four foot high wasp. Because wasps are only ever going to be advertised with a view to their destruction, it is very clear from a single glance exactly what my client's business is. Gary should also have his overalls, tee-shirts, sweat-shirts, etc, heavily branded with his company name, logo, web-site address and phone number etc.

Simon's Marketing

Simon's market is at the very least nationwide and quite possibly international. Simon's customers are exclusively the owners of golf courses.

Simon's marketing challenges are very, very different from each of the three other characters. His product is unknown and therefore there is zero chance of someone searching him out on a whim. The good news for Simon is that he knows exactly who his target market is and where to find them. The other good news is that golf clubs are not the most dynamic and busy of environments and there is a very good chance that Simon will get an audience with the chief executive of the club to explain his software.

Simon has been playing at his local club since he was very small and knows all the influential people within that club. Whilst he has been working at his job he has also persuaded his local club to try out his software, free of charge. The club have agreed to sign a non-disclosure agreement, (as the last thing Simon needs is someone stealing his ideas at this early stage). Simon should make sure he gets as much protection for his product as he can either by patenting it and/or getting a trade mark. There are many agencies who can advise him on this and a simple search on Google will tell him where to go and who to talk to. The simple concept behind Simon's software is that most golf courses are underutilised, and if his software could make sure that all of the club's playing slots are used without endangering the quality of the course and access to the course for the members, then the club can increase its revenue. Once the product has been fully tested at his local club, Simon will be ready to market it. On the assumption that it has been an unqualified success, Simon should ensure that he gets a testimonial from the chief executive of the club which will help him market it further. He should launch his website at that point (and not before) along with a video (see V for Video) and also all the necessary search engine optimisation (also see later item on this topic).

There are a number of magazines that golf club owners would read and Simon should seriously consider taking out an ad in one of these magazines. The ad needs to be big enough to be noticed and needs to be very direct and clear in what it promises to do. The success of this form of advertising, known as space ads, is very hit and miss, but in the early days of launching his product it is definitely an avenue that is worth exploring. If he gets no response at all then he knows that space ads are not going to work for his particular product.

There are exhibitions held throughout the UK that specialise in all manner of golf products e.g. the London Golf Show. It is highly recommended that Simon attends as many of these exhibitions as he can and further should book himself a stall at these exhibitions. A combination of the space ads and putting himself at the exhibitions is likely to result in at least a few meetings but, Simon should not rely on these to launch his product.

The very best way Simon can launch his product successfully is by visiting golf clubs himself and demonstrating the software one to one with the club's owner or manager. Simon could employ a salesman to do this job and this may be something he would consider later on, but no-one is going to have the passion and expertise for this product that he has and he knows the product works because he's tested it out at his local club. Once he sits down in front of someone, he can get that passion across.

So how does he get himself in front of these prospects?

He could cold call, and because of the nature of golf clubs and the fact that many people do have time on their hands he will achieve some success in doing so. A better way would be to first of all introduce himself to the prospect by sending them a letter and some promotional material explaining the product in clear and concise terms. In the letter he will say that he will be calling them as a matter of courtesy to check that they have received the material. Once he makes the phone call he will ask for an appointment so that he can demonstrate the software. Simon needs to get himself into a situation where he's making two or three visits per day so that he can hone his presentation of the product. Simon will definitely need to get the expertise of a design and/or advertising agency to help him with his branding, space ads and web-site. All of this needn't cost the earth, but in order to be done properly he should be budgeting on probably not less than £10,000.

"And this is the exact point we put Scruffy in charge of marketing and sales."

Chris's Marketing

Chris's market covers a large area, but I would suggest probably no more than 50 miles, as Chris has got to get to the client's premises within a fairly short period of time. His customers will be mainly small businesses but may also include home users of computers.

The problem that Chris has is convincing his target market of his expertise. There are very few nationally recognised qualifications and training programmes, at the moment anyway, in the field of computing. This is a world that is full of 'so called' experts which has led to a good deal of scepticism and confusion. For most people switching on the PC is the beginning and end of their technical knowledge when it comes to computers. Just in the same way with cars as people have no idea what's happening "under the bonnet". Referral and word of mouth is therefore how Chris is going to get people to use his services. Networking groups are an obvious first choice for him and he should attend as many of these as he can. Eventually there is going to be someone attending a networking event whose computer or computer systems have failed on that very day. Chris has got an excellent chance of being the person hired to solve that problem, as this is the sort of problem that generally cannot wait around too long before it is fixed. If Chris does a good job he is likely to be remembered and possibly even retained by that individual. Chris should take every opportunity possible to emphasise his expertise by giving talks and seminars at the networking groups he goes to and also taking any opportunity at business exhibitions to do the same. For example, this could be a very simple 20 minute presentation on what to look out for with the latest version of windows or, the advantages of one data base product over another data base product. A public speaking course would benefit Chris enormously as providing he can muster the bravery to stand up in front of people, he has much to gain.

"I think we should have a word with Bob about his sales technique."

For lots more information about marketing which is completely free, visit the Chartered Institute of Marketing's website on **www.CIM.co.uk**

M... is for Mistakes

You will make them, of that there is absolutely no doubt. Heather will undoubtedly have her hairdressing disasters and a customer will leave her shop somewhat crestfallen. Heather must learn, and undoubtedly she has already learnt, by the look on the customers face when such a disaster has in fact occurred. Customers will rarely lose their temper when such things happen, you will just never hear from them again. You must learn to read the signals of when a mistake has been made and then you must act. The first thing to do is take all the blame, admit the mistake and tell the customer you are going to rectify it forthwith. Maybe the customer didn't give Heather the right instructions, or clear enough instructions, and the resultant hairstyle is not 100% Heather's fault. That is completely irrelevant! Heather must take the blame completely. She must tell the customer that not only will she not be charging her for the haircut she will also receive the next one free of charge. As I've already explained above, repeat business is what is going to make Heather successful so she must at all costs make sure that this unhappy customer returns.

N

N... is for Networking

One of the best developments in British business over the last few decades is networking groups. They are an inexpensive and easy way of promoting your business and also developing your understanding of other businesses. Both of these aspects are to my mind of equal importance. A simple Google search of networking groups in whatever area you're in will reveal a plethora of organisations from Chambers of Commerce to groups that specialise in everything from eco commerce to women only groups. There are people who have bad things to say about networking groups, but this is normally because they approach them with the wrong attitude. These are the people who will have attended one networking group, handed out a swathe of business cards and promotional literature and for their efforts they receive not one single phone call. The reality is that this is pretty normal and sometimes the best result you get out of a networking group is an invitation to another networking group, but really you should approach networking as a means of gathering information rather than an opportunity to sell your business.

There is an expression called 'giver's gain' or to put it another way 'give to get'. An example of this would be where a friend of yours has mentioned to you that they are having an extension on their house and they need an architect. The very next day you are attending a local networking group and there are various professionals there but you notice on the attendance list that there is going to be an architect at the meeting. You have not met this person but you have a reason to introduce yourself to them. So you introduce yourself to them and explain your friend's situation and before you know it you're in a good conversation about business generally. You take that person's card, you hand it to your friend and you've done everyone a favour. What you cannot do of course is to recommend that architect as someone who is good at their job, because you do not yet know this fact! Please see R for Referrals later in the book. This does not mean that the contact is not of use but it means that you must treat that contact with caution. You say to your friend "this is someone I've met who may be of use to you".

At some point at the meeting you will be asked what you do for a living and at that point you should tell your audience what it is that you do in a succinct and non-salesey way as possible. You will see many people around you doing exactly the opposite and boring everybody to death in the process. If the person standing opposite you needs your services they will say so pretty quickly otherwise don't overdo it. Be sure to talk to as many people as possible and ask them questions about their business. This is not just simple politeness but also the more you know about other businesses the better you will be at your own.

Networking events generally cost anything between £10-20 per event and would normally involve either a breakfast or drinks and canapés depending on which end of the day the meeting takes place. Be open minded about which ones you join, clearly if you are male, a women only Group is going to be a bit of a challenge, but don't rule out something that you have no interest in. You will almost certainly learn something by being there.

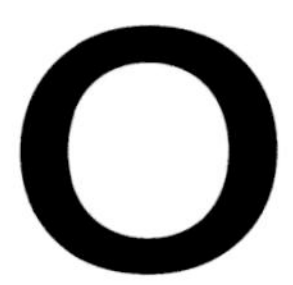

O... is for Opportunity

Opportunities need to be evaluated very closely. What sometimes can look like an excellent opportunity can turn out to be a mill stone.

Chris having just set up his business is lucky enough to receive two offers in his first week! Lucky Chris. The first is from a company who wants to have Chris as their in-house IT consultant for four days a week and for this they would pay £50K per year. Bearing in mind that Chris' salary at his old company was £35K per year, and a self-employed income of £50K is equivalent to an employed salary of £60K, Chris has nearly doubled his income in his first week!

The other offer Chris has is for two days consultancy per month which in a full year will pay just over £14K. So which offer should Chris take?

The first job when analysed, works out at a day rate of less than £250. The second job has a day rate of £600. For someone of Chris' expertise he should be looking at a day rate of £500 at the very least. The problem with accepting the first offer is that it's going to tie Chris down virtually full time. He will only have one day left a week in which to offer his services to other people and that is not an awful lot of room to manoeuvre. If things go wrong at this company, he is right back where he started.

The other offer is at a day rate which is realistic and commercial and if Chris does a good job for them he will definitely be recommended on to other companies. If he can fill his time with this day rate his annual income will be more like £150K per year.

P... is for Promises

Keep them... That's all you need to know.

It doesn't matter that you've woken up and are feeling like death from a cold, or whether you've just been told by someone that a dear relative is gravely ill. Whatever the reason is, if you've promised your customer that you are going to do something make sure you do it.

When you were an employee you could have got away with not doing it and everybody would have understood, but you are no longer that person and your success depends on delivering on your promises.

P... is for Planning

It is often said that one of the major reasons that British businesses have failed in the past is that they do not plan for the long term, and you should not make that mistake.

Gary is given the opportunity of a meeting with a building contractor who he knows is not in the market for using his services in the near future. Should he go to that meeting if he's not going to get immediate business? He should see this as a golden opportunity! An opportunity to impress upon that contractor his personality and expertise. Sometime after the meeting he should thank the contractor for seeing him and on a quarterly basis send him an e-mail to ask how business is going and to enquire as to whether there are any opportunities coming up for him. There is nothing to be lost by this and in the fullness of time he may well find that the contractor will put business his way.

P... is for Prioritising

On any given day you know that you have a number of tasks to do. You have made your 'to do list' from the previous day and you have ten or so tasks that you know you've got to get done on that day... and that's even before you've set to on meeting your clients' requirements.

One of those jobs is a nasty one.

Chris has been sent a very detailed specification for a new PC network that a client needs very soon. It's a big order and Chris does not want to mess it up, but he is really only confident on about 80% of what he's being asked to do. He does know however, where he can start doing the research on the remaining 20% and that research is the nasty one on today's to do list.

There is an acronym known as BANJOE which is Bang A Nasty Job Out Early. This is all about jumping on your to do list and going for the nastiest one first. Some people can do this and best of luck to them if they can, but speaking personally it is not something I can do. I think the longer Chris thinks about that particular nasty job, the longer he will remain on the sofa watching breakfast telly. Also on his to do list is a follow up e-mail that he must send to a client to ask them whether everything is ok with the network repairs he did last week. Now this isn't a complicated job to do, it involves just shooting out a couple of lines to the client on an e-mail - estimated time 45 seconds from beginning to end. He also has an e-mail he must send to another supplier asking for a quote for four bits of equipment that he has ordered from this supplier before. Total time taken for that job, 45 seconds. So Chris can make a start on those two easy jobs straight away, no thought required. That's two out of his ten jobs done and then he can move through the rest of the list and by the time is half way through his brain is motoring, he's moving through the gears and I reckon by the time he gets to the nasty one somehow it will all seem a lot easier. So in short, it doesn't matter, in my view, which of those jobs on Chris's 'to do list' is done first. The important thing is to start. Action is the key.

P... is for Paying Staff

Generally speaking staff should not be either paid too much or too little. Just like Goldilocks, you want to achieve something that is just right. There are unfortunate consequences from either paying too much or too little.

It may appear on the face of it to be economically advantageous for you to pay your staff at the lower end of what the market has determined (what the market has determined can be found out from recruitment consultants or by looking at job advertisements e.g. monster.co.uk is a good resource for this). There are certainly some employers who can get away with paying their staff very little and also retaining the staff loyalty. These organisations tend to be highly prestigious companies who are market leaders. In these instances employees will seek out opportunities to work for them whilst they're training, irrespective of how little they are being paid. This is certainly not the case for any of our four characters and therefore the likelihood is that they will need to be paying above the average to get any calibre of staff at all. If you pay your staff too much then they will run out of motivation for working any harder. You definitely will need to keep the financial carrot just dangling in front of their noses so that they have something to work towards.

P... is for Pricing

The price at which you sell your products or services is going to be largely determined by what your competitors do. This is true for all of our characters except for Simon, whose product is unique. As we have seen from the marketing section, Simon has first of all decided to test his product free of charge at his

local golf club. Once the testing of that product has been completed and that particular customer is happy that it works and is increasing his turnover it would be worth asking that customer how much they would have paid for the product had they known how successful it was going to be. The particular customer should feel comfortable doing this as they've got it for nothing! This is at least a start point for Simon in determining how much to market his product for. Unlike the other three characters Simon's product has very little variable cost attached to it. There is also no competition for his product, but the usage of this product could increase a golf club's annual income by up to £100K per annum. (He knows this having analysed the underutilisation at his local club and extrapolating that across various clubs in the County). Simon estimates that a club would be unlikely to get an income increase of less than £10,000. In other words he estimates the extra income that the club would generate to be between £10,000 - £100,000 per year. How much they actually make would depend on a number of factors, including the number of members on the golf course, the maintenance programme, how well the course is rated by golf users, etc.

Golf club owners would be unwilling to pay an amount for this product that exceeds their likely annual increase in turnover, so already we know that Simon cannot price this product at anything above £10,000. Simon will probably wish to price the product at something between £1,000 - £5,000 for a one-off purchase, but more importantly he will wish to charge the club owner an on-going annual licence and support fee of between £200 - £500 per year. This is what is called residual income and in the long run will be what drives the profitability of Simon's business.

P... is for Partners

I have had the misfortune to watch many partnerships fall apart, and believe me when that happens it is extremely painful for all concerned. There is a huge temptation to start the business in a partnership, After all who wants to be alone?

You have to ask yourself what your partner will bring to the business, do they have the same desire as you? Are you doing it just because they're a mate? More importantly do they have the same vision as you? Remember if the business does succeed, the fruits of your labours will be divided into two which means that the business needs to be able to produce at least twice what it would have done had you been alone. The key word here is synergy. This is a situation where effectively one plus one equals three, and if there is synergy between you and your partner – fantastic! That's the goose that lays the golden eggs. In my experience, however, most partnerships are one plus one equals one and a half... which is, of course, a road to ruin.

Q... is for Quotes

Whether it's Heather or Chris or Gary, if a customer asks for a quote for a job it is vital that the resultant cost of the job bears a close similarity to the original quote. Nothing annoys customers more than being told "Oh, Madam it will cost you such and such" but by the end of the job it is three times that sum. This could be particularly true for Gary who may well find that the problem is much more extensive than he first diagnosed and the resultant cost may well be much, much more than the quote. Before he goes any further he must inform the customer of this and let the customer make the decision whether they intend to hire him to fix it at that moment, or to leave it for another day.

R... is for Referrals

Referrals are absolutely the best way of growing your business, and the important thing about referrals is that they cannot be forced. There are people who will tell you that you can build a referral 'system'. This is not only alien to us British people, it is also rather fraudulent in my view. If people like the service or product that you deliver they are almost certain to tell other people about it and don't need to be forced to do so.

Similarly, you should be free and easy with the referrals that you hand out for businesses that have supplied you. The caveat to this, of course, is that you must be free and easy with your referrals only for businesses that are good. Do not, under any circumstances, recommend someone who is not good, as this will rebound back to you, in an unpleasant way. Shout from the rooftops about businesses that have done good things for you and you can be sure that this will come back to you tenfold at some stage later on. It is a very naturally British thing to be good at selling other people and be poor at selling yourself. This is not something that you should be in any way afraid of, as in the process of selling other people eventually you will find that some people are selling you.

R... Is for Risk

Risk is the one word which separates the entrepreneur from the rest of the population. If you are not comfortable with a certain element of risk, you have no business being in business.

By the time we are adults of all us have an in-built risk monitor which tells us whether we are risk adverse or risk tolerant. We are not talking about the kind of risk that puts everything on black, but we are talking about a level of risk tolerance that enables financial decisions to be made where the outcome is uncertain.

It is definitely one of the first questions you should ask yourself if you are about to set up in business.

People often consider self-employed people to be at more risk than employed people. One thing that can be said in reply to that is that a self-employed person will have several streams of income from several customers and therefore if one of those customers or clients ceases to be, they will still have an income from the remainder. The employed person has one source of income... and that seems a lot riskier to me!

R... is for Ruthless

A commonly held belief is that to be successful in business you have to be a ruthless person, or adopt a ruthless persona. Nothing in fact could be further from the truth.

Real life is not like Dragons Den or The Apprentice. Pointing at your staff and screaming 'You're fired' is unlikely to endear you to your workforce. Humiliating employees, suppliers (and perish the thought customers) is going to get you absolutely no-where. An excellent phrase to remember here is 'what goes around comes around', and if anybody has been on the sharp end of your new found ruthlessness, they will be sure to remember it.

R... is for Resilience

Resilience is the ability to recover from a set-back. We all know people who once they get a knock-back of some form will spend the next two days in bed moping about it. If you are that kind of person then I'm afraid you will find owning your own business probably too much of a struggle. We also conversely know those individuals who don't seem to let anything get them down. The problems they come across are like water off the proverbial duck's back. These individuals have a personal characteristic that is so important in surviving in business, and in fact I would say that of all the personal characteristics you should ideally have to run a business this is one of the most important. Gary is one such individual and his irrepressible enthusiasm and general joy of life is, on the one hand intensely annoying but is also infectiously endearing.

Gary has had a very bruising encounter with the 70 year old Mrs Jones but he won't let this get him down. This will just end up being an amusing story to tell to his mates in the pub later on AND more importantly Gary is also someone who can learn from his mistakes. Bringing these two characteristics together makes Gary a candidate for success.

Simon on the other hand is not so resilient after a recent meeting with the Chief Executive at a target golf club. Simon knows the meeting did not go well. He will go through the normal procedures of following up the meeting by e-mail but he has a feeling in the pit of his stomach that he is going to get rejected. This is not the first time that he has been knocked-back and he knows what will happen next. He will go back to his house, sit in front of his computer and mope for the next two hours. This is part of who Simon is and at the moment there is nothing he can do about that. What he needs to do is find himself a routine to shake him out of those two hours of self introspection. This could be something as simple as going down the gym to shake all the bad thoughts out of his system, or it could be meeting his girlfriend for lunch – something to break the routine, to bring him back to his required levels of energy and enthusiasm.

S

"Of course, I do have a very supportive wife."

S... is for Spouses

Spouses are of course a vital part of your business and a vital part of your success. I'm not recommending that you rush to get married if you're not already married, but what I can say is that it is a very tax efficient thing to do particularly if you have a limited company. Your accountant should advise you on this matter.

HMRC has in the past poked its nose into tax and family businesses and lost a famous case quite recently, and quite rightly so. The case was called The Arctic Systems case and it was ultimately ruled that wives and husbands have a vital role to play in the business even though they are not doing the day to day nuts and bolts (actually that is just my interpretation of the case but it is definitely true). Do ask your accountant about making your spouse a director and shareholder. It is not always a good idea to do so, but it is a question that should be asked.

S... is for Success

Clearly, you have set up your own business to be a success but we really should define what success means so that you will know what it is when you get there. It should be partly financial but is also much more to do with a sense of independence and knowing that your destiny can be determined by you and you alone. Clearly, in financial terms, if your business is not going to provide you with an income at least as great as that when you were employed, then it is not a success.

Success is not necessarily being one of the super rich. Let's face it most of us are never going to be super rich and in reality most of us are not prepared to make the sacrifice required to get to that stage. In summary therefore, if you have left your job to set up a business and if that business is bringing you, within two years an income that is greater than that earned while working for someone else then you can count that as a success. Anything greater than that, of course, is a bigger success!

S... is for Speaking in Public

Most of us would rather eat mud than stand up and speak in public. This fact is undoubtedly true and the flip side of this fact is that we tend to hold those who can speak in public in very high regard. People who are confident about speaking in public are people we tend to think of as being experts and we are suitably impressed by their confidence and delivery.

The good news is that although some people are naturally good at speaking in public this is something that can be learnt by anyone. There is no magic trick to speaking well in public. It is all down to rehearsal, rehearsal and more rehearsal, speaking clearly and most of all speaking slowly. If you are asked to speak for five minutes make sure that your rehearsals are such that they are timed for five minutes, no longer and no shorter.

Will Heather gain much from standing up in front of people and talking about the latest hair colouring techniques? Well, possibly not, but for the other three it is definitely something that will be of great use to them. The opportunities to do this exist in networking groups and also at business exhibitions. If there is an opportunity to do it, it should be taken. There is very little downside, and much to be gained.

S... is for Suppliers

Be good to your suppliers if they are good to you. Make sure that you pay them on time, but do not give them any leeway for poor service or poor delivery. Over time your suppliers may consider you a solid, grateful customer and in so being they may wish to push up your prices. This sounds rather cynical but be aware that it does happen. Be honest and open with your suppliers and do not be afraid to challenge their prices, particularly where you know for a fact that a competitor is offering a lower price.

In the long run it is better to form a good relationship with one supplier for a product than to have many suppliers for the same product.

Be wary of suppliers who tell you that they want to "partner" with you. At the time of writing this is a popular expression, which indicates that the supplier wishes to form a business relationship with you which he's referring to as partnership. In reality a partnership is one where two parties set out on a joint venture and share the risk in that venture. The relationship between you and your supplier is not that relationship. If someone says to you that they wish to partner with you thank them for it and say...

"Well in that case, as you are clearly wishing to become a partner in this commercial venture (even though you are only going to buy a few bits and pieces of stationery from them) you will wish to share the risk on this and I may or may not pay you, I will see how it goes".

There will be a long silence on the other end of the line at this point...

T... is for Twitter

Is Twitter for twits? At the time of writing I think it is too early to say if it's a useful business tool or a very useful way of wasting your precious time. What is almost certainly true is that there is a burgeoning industry of people who are writing about how to use Twitter.

Remember... you are NOT Stephen Fry. Clearly, if you are an entertainer of any kind it makes perfect sense to have a means of communicating what you are up to, whether that be a forthcoming show, new release etc.

I question if you were a plumber whether this would be entirely appropriate. Sending out tweets regarding today's news about 'developments in u-bend technology'... not exactly a riveting read. The other new media way of marketing is Facebook. I think this could be useful for certain businesses, but for most people I expect it would be a waste of time. The last thing you want to do is look like you are jumping on the latest bandwagon, especially one which is after all mostly about friendships not business. Remember these are only just ways of getting in touch with people.

Getting in touch with lots of people all at once to inform them of an impending event is very much what Twitter and Facebook is very good at, particularly Twitter. As we know from the golf software engineer, he is designing his programme to work closely with Twitter. His programme will shoot out messages to potential buyers of golf rounds who will be constantly updated of the prices of the rounds and of the availability of the slots.

Heather is someone else that may well be able to utilise Twitter to her advantage, providing she ensures it doesn't take up too much of her time. Clearly, Heather is going to want to spend as much time as possible with some scissors in her hand rather than a laptop on her knee. Twitter is a very good way of starting a conversation about a hot topic, or maybe even the latest hairstyle. We all remember when Jennifer Aniston from the Friends series had that famous haircut. Heather keeps herself abreast of what is happening in fashion and she could do no worse than offer her views on what is happening through Twitter. Heather will be keen to develop the idea within her clients' minds that she knows all about the latest styles and trends.

T... Is for Talent

Your business is going to be grown initially based on your talent alone. In the fullness of time as you get busier and want to take the business on further, the business will grow based on the talents of your employees. Spotting talent is an art, but if you get it right the benefits are enormous.

You need to be flexible about where the talent may be found. When people think of the word talent they generally think of young people, but in reality talent could be found in any age group. Gary's business has expanded rapidly and he can't be looking at gas boilers in several houses all at once. He needs to find himself someone he can delegate to. His first thought of course is to hire a young apprentice, but that may not be the best solution for him. How about someone who has recently retired or sold up their business but is looking for a few part time hours? They have a wealth of experience and knowledge of customers and are unlikely to be as demanding as a younger apprentice. The young tend to be hungrier for success and tend to be able to learn processes and tasks much quicker than older people. The disadvantages of younger people are that due to lack of experience they tend to not cope so well when things go wrong and tend not to have the same level of interpersonal skills that an older person might have.

Talent needs to be nurtured, it needs to be rewarded, it needs to be (if applicable) promoted. Promotions will always be more effective if done from within your firm. Do not be surprised at how much good people can cope with. If you have someone in your business who is enthusiastic, bright and driven, then promote them! Promote them into areas where they have very little experience, as the key determinates for success are drive, enthusiasm and intelligence and you will get much greater success by giving one of your existing team a shot at that problem rather than trying to find the right person from the employment market.

U

U... is for Unreasonable People

The good news about people is that most people are reasonable. Certainly in my experience of dealing with many, many clients, at least 95% of all people that you meet are going to be reasonable people. Reasonable, rational, logical people who will do as they are done to.

There are however, unreasonable people out there, people who are irrational and unpredictable. These people should be avoided. One thing you should know about these people is that they are unreasonable on a consistent basis. They don't decide to take the weekend off from being unreasonable. They will suck the life blood out of you and even if they are your only client they should be avoided at all costs as they will hold you back from fulfilling your full potential.

V

V... is for VAT

VAT is something much misunderstood by people who are not in business. The mere mention of the word strikes fear in the ignorant. In reality there really is very little to fear from the VAT man. At the time of writing VAT registration is compulsory for businesses turning over more than £70,000 and it is voluntary for those that are turning over less. If your entire customer base are people who are not themselves registered for VAT then clearly the longer you remain unregistered for VAT the more competitive you are going to be. If all of your client base are companies that are themselves VAT registered the fact that you are adding VAT on is irrelevant to them and is a non-cost. Both Chris and Simon should register for VAT for another reason and that is credibility. A business that is unregistered for VAT is definitely turning over less than £70,000. A business that is registered for VAT may or may not be turning over that amount but would either Chris or Simon be willing to be that open about the size of their companies?

Being registered for VAT is, surprisingly, something that can make you money. I know that sounds like a peculiar thing to say, but some years ago the Government introduced the Flat Rate Scheme to encourage people to get their VAT returns correct. To incentivise people to do that basically they built in a giveaway that is equivalent to anything between £1,000 and £4,000 a year. This, of course, sounds completely mad, but is absolutely true and you should most definitely ask your accountant about it.

V... is for Videos

Videos are incredibly cheap to make now and are potentially a great way to advertise your business on your web-site. Videos on web-sites can help you explain your products and services in a way that will engage the viewer in a more personable and immediate sense... if done well. If done badly they could make you look like a total idiot.

Gary, whose girlfriend loves him dearly, has a face like a bag of spanners. He does not look good in photographs and he certainly does not look good on a video. It's questionable whether Gary explaining what a boiler does on a video is going to be any more exciting than explaining it in print, and Gary's got a good chance of blowing everything altogether if he puts his face on a video. However, one of the most popular searches on YouTube is 'How do I..." and Gary, despite his facial and sartorial limitations, may think about utilising his infectious enthusiasm to give short videos about how to bleed a radiator, how to perform basic maintenance on your central heating system, etc. Apart from giving away vital information for nothing, in so going Gary is putting himself forward as an expert.

It is an entirely different proposition I think for Simon. Simon does not have a particularly good presence in front of a camera, but is extremely enthusiastic about his software. If he explained it face to camera with a blank wall behind him, the chances are that he could get himself tied up in knots in software gobbledygook. On the other hand, if Simon was to take himself on to a golf course and stand by the first tee, he then has a better chance of explaining in very graphic terms what his software does. He could, for instance, be filmed on the first tee with no-one teeing off, he could come back a quarter of an hour later, stand at the first tee, again no-one teeing off. In this way he could illustrate the opportunity that the Golf Club is wasting and how his software can help fill those empty slots.

V… is for Vision

Vision sounds like it good be another one of those jargon words that we can all lose ourselves in. Vision is really a technicolour version of goals (See G for Goals). Whereas goals are black and white, often expressed in numbers and are one dimensional, a vision is the filled in, full colour version of where you want to be in one year, two years, three years' time.

This vision will say in Heather's case, include an idea of what her hairdressing salon is going to look like, how she is going to be greeting her customers, how they are going to be congratulating her on the great job that she's doing. In Simon's case this will be a vision of his software being installed in golf clubs all around the country and how those golf clubs are going to benefit and make more money by installing his software. Vision is important because it is a great motivator. It helps you to get out of bed in the morning, it reinforces why you are doing all this, why you are creating something out of nothing. The vision at the moment is only that, and you are going to turn that vision into reality.

W... is for Window of Opportunity

It is an old adage, but one that is undoubtedly true, "the window of opportunity will always open at the most inopportune moment". This is a sub-section of sod's law. Sod's law dictates that if an event is going to happen it will almost always happen at the most inconvenient moment.

Heather has told her local estate agent that she is looking for a shop on the high street and the agent is to let her know as soon as one becomes available. The agent has told her that in the normal course of events it will be 18 months at the very earliest and 4 years at the latest before a shop comes up on her particular high street. Eighteen months is ok as that fits in with Heather's budgeting.

However... not two weeks after that conversation the agent calls up and says we have got just what you're looking for but unfortunately it's available now! Heather cannot afford it now. What should Heather do?

In my opinion Heather must beg, borrow and sell her possessions in order to get that shop. The likelihood of her getting that opportunity right at the moment when she really wants it is slim. The timing is, of course, completely wrong, but it is the right opportunity. It is the opportunity that is much more important than the timing, and the opportunity must be taken.

W... is for What Not to Wear

Gary wears his hair slicked back but slightly pushed up at the front, which neatly compliments his quarter inch stubble. Gary is very pleased with his look and so particularly is his girlfriend. Seventy year old Mrs Jones however, whose boiler is going to be fixed by Gary tomorrow, sees a man with funny hair who hasn't bothered to shave. Mrs Jones thinks that if Gary hasn't bothered to shave, Gary might not be too bothered about fixing her boiler properly.

Mrs Jones is not up to speed with the latest fashions in hair and stubble, but she must not be criticised for that, for she is the customer. In short, wear neutral, appropriate attire.

W... is for Web-Site

Even ten years ago, people were saying that web-sites were a luxury and not a necessity. This has now firmly changed, and I believe all four of our characters will need a web-site. Heather's web-site needn't be that sophisticated but will be a way that she can get across her personality, style and method alongside giving the normal information about where she is, what she does and how much her services cost. Most people will be pointed to Heather's shop by knowing that it already exists on the high street, but that's not to say that others will not wish to search out her services through the internet.

Gary's web-site needs to be much more sophisticated. He needs to optimise his web-site so that he can be found easily. This technique is known as search engine optimisation and there are any number of "experts" who can advise on this. Some of these experts, of course, are no more than charlatans, and care must be taken, but there are courses available for a few hundred pounds where Gary can be taught what words to put in his web-site that will enable him to be found quickly by those seeking his services. Gary should also consider Google Ad Words (See G for Google Ad Words).

Chris's web-site needs to be something similar to Heathers at the very least, but will probably need to go into more detail about his areas of expertise. Again, he will wish to take advantage of search engine optimisation so that he can be found, particularly if he has specialist knowledge in particular areas.

Simon's web-site is probably going to be the most sophisticated of all. Simon should very seriously consider the use of video in his web-site (see V for Video) as that will be a very powerful tool to enable Simon to get across quite a complicated idea in very visual terms. Simon's web-site must emphasise the unique and exclusive nature of his product and therefore must be of the highest quality. Anyone coming onto Simon's site must leave it with the impression that they have just been let into a very big secret.

Web-sites at the time of writing will cost anything between £1,000 - £5,000 depending on sophistication and I suggest Heather would be at one end of that price spectrum and Simon at the other.

W... is for Wages (Minimum)

A very small bureaucratic fact that you need to be aware of is that there is a current minimum wage in force in this Country, and at the time of writing this is £5.93 for an adult of 21 and over, it changes annually. (From 1 October 2011 it changes from £5.93 to £6.08). Don't make the mistake of paying less than this, as this could prove very painful for all concerned.

W... is for WIIFM (Pronounced WIFFUM)

WIIFM stands for 'WHAT'S IN IT FOR ME'. This is the basis of all commercial transactions in the history of the human race.

No-one will part with any money before this particular question has been answered.

For you the entrepreneur this means that you must always think from the customers' perspective. Why should the customer spend an extra £10 to have their hair cut by Heather? They can get a perfectly good haircut five shops down the road. Heather must make a compelling case to make that customer spend the extra £10.

WIIFM is a question easily answered in the cases of Gary and Chris, as they will be remedying a very pressing problem.

For Simon, of course, answering this particular question is a very key part of his sales pitch. What's in it for the golf course owners is, in short, more revenue. The reason there is going to be more revenue is because of more efficient utilisation of the golf course.

X... is for Excuses (Yes, a Small Spelling Cheat Here)

Excuses are for employees - they are not the preserve of the self-employed.

You have just entered into the world of no excuses.

The only person to blame for anything going wrong is you. You can make all the excuses you like but in the end you are only fooling yourself.

Y... is for Yes

The power of YES. Americans make a great play of the positive attitude and the power of yes. Despite what we may think of the Americans, they have a very good point. Customers want to hear your positive thoughts, your positive inputs, your positive responses to their questions. Try to always think yes, rather than putting up barriers to how a solution may be reached.

What a customer wants to hear is "Don't worry I'll take care of that".

Z

Z… is for ZZZ's Sleep

An owner of a famous greetings card company once stood up to give a speech to young entrepreneurs. "Sleep" he said, and then paused – "7 hours for men, 8 hours for women and more for fools". Well, if he is right I must be one of the bigger fools, as I need in excess of 8 hours sleep every night.

If you're one of the lucky ones who needs less sleep then good for you! In theory you can do an awful lot more with your day than those who need more sleep. The one thing you must remember is that you cannot train yourself to have less sleep than you need.

The amount of sleep you need… is the amount of sleep you need.

Whatever it is make sure that you get it, because running your own business is going to require every ounce of stamina that you possess. Do not, under any circumstances, listen to fools who will tell you you can get by on less sleep.

AFTERWORD

So I hope you have found this book to be informative at the very least. If you haven't set up your business yet, nothing would please me more if this book motivated you to go out and do it now.

So where are those annoying e-mails from your boss telling you to do a million, trivial things that will waste yours and everybody else's time? Well, that boss has now gone, never to return, you have a new boss now... YOU! Your new boss is the toughest, most exacting and most demanding you will ever have.

With that force behind you, how can you fail? Now, go and make some money!